TABLE OF

For [...] [...]ected to God through writing and journaling. Many writings by Christians [...] [...]e still revered and studied today. But not everyone expresses himself or herself best with words. And even the finest wordsmiths have occasions when they can't find the right word or phrase for a certain situation. For many of us, there are times when we express ourselves best through doodles, pictures, and scribbles.

Doodle Discipleship

The BOOK OF FIDGETS is an invitation to doodle discipleship. It gives every young Christian who has ever filled a worship bulletin or Sunday school handout with pictures and patterns space to express herself or himself, respond to God, engage Scripture, and explore what it means to be a follower of Christ.

While the BOOK OF FIDGETS aims to provide a sacred space for doodling, there is no reason that you cannot write in the BOOK OF FIDGETS. If you feel more comfortable expressing ideas in words than in pictures, you are free to do so.

This book can be used as a personal journal, or groups can work through it together using the free leader's guide available at www.AbingdonPress.com/BookofFidgets.

Become an Animator

You will notice an empty box in the bottom corner of each page. This space is set aside for you to turn the BOOK OF FIDGETS into a flipbook. Making a flipbook is a simple form of animation. Here's how it works: Draw a person or object in one box. Then draw the same person or object in the next box with some small change. For instance, a person might have lifted an arm or moved slightly to the right. Continue to draw pictures with subtle changes. When you flip through the pictures quickly, they will appear to move, like a cartoon.

The BOOK OF FIDGETS allows you to create two flipbooks: one on the right-hand pages and one on the left-hand pages. When you flip through the book from front to back, you will see the pictures on the bottom corner of the right-hand pages. When you flip from back to front, you will see what you've drawn on the left-hand pages.

If you need help getting started, videos of flipbooks and instructions and suggestions for creating them are easy to find on the Internet.

Express Yourself

Each page of this book gives you instructions or suggestions for what to draw or write. Some instructions are open-ended; others are more specific. Some of the doodle prompts involve exploring and learning about yourself. Some teach you about Scripture, Christian belief, and Christian traditions. Some invite you to pray. Some invite you to act.

In between the sections in this book you will see "Free Doodle Spaces." These pages have no instructions and no rules. Fill them however you would like.

Regardless of the activity or what the instructions suggest that you do, always focus on three things whenever you're sketching, scribbling, or scrawling in the Book of Fidgets:

1. Be creative.

2. Connect with God.

3. Have fun.

This book belongs to:

Doodle your name.

Write your name very neatly.

Scribble your name.

Give yourself a nickname and write it here.

Doodle Your Heart Out

Be creative. Connect with God.
Have fun!

Doodle around the holes.

Write next to each hole something that is missing from your life!

Put Your → Fingerprints

Using dirt, makeup, lipstick, or whatever **Doodle** images around the fingerprints that express what makes you special.

BELOW

Inside Each Circle

doodle ways God has blessed you.

Doodle yourself as A Superhero

Doodle the gifts that God has given your Superhero (you).

what makes you happy in life?

MUSIC

DANCE

DOODLE LIKE A SKYDIVER!

Scribble, scrawl, and scratch all over the page.

How does God bring order out of chaos?

HOW does it feel to be out of control?

Good   BAD

Don't Know

If GOD wrote you a check for $10,000,
what would you do with it???

Doodle or write below.

GOD COFFEE love DANCE STAR MUSIC

♪ Love ♪♪

DOODLE all the things that make U who U are.

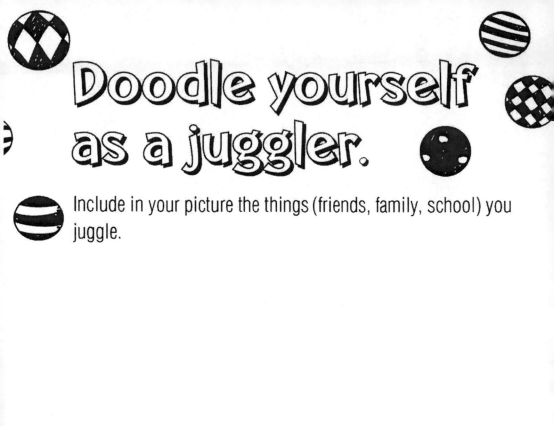

Doodle yourself as a juggler.

Include in your picture the things (friends, family, school) you juggle.

who is the most beautiful person you know?

Draw or write below.

List the 5 things that make that person beautiful.

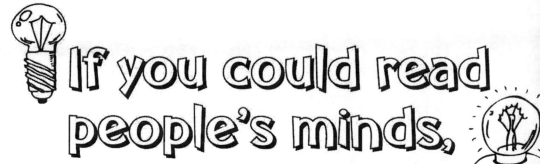

If you could read people's minds,

what would you want to know?

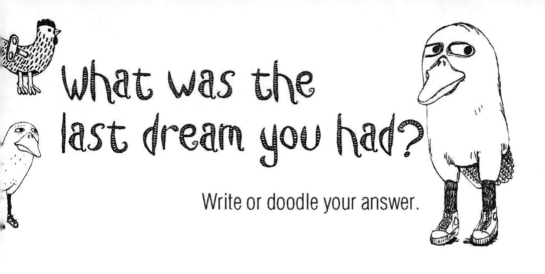

What was the last dream you had?

Write or doodle your answer.

Has God ever spoken to you in your dreams?

Doodle what's on your mind.

Doodle an object.

Doodle something that changes into something else.

What is the stupidest thing someone has dared you to do?

Think about the last time you were mad. Doodle yourself as an angry monster.

Doodle with the hand you normally don't write with.

Then list 5 things you like to do but often feel uncomfortable doing.

1.
2.
3.
4.
5.

Do you have a secret talent? Doodle yourself doing it.

GOD

In what ways does God affect your life?

Write or doodle your answer.

Draw or list your favorite things. Then go without one of those things for one day.

How hard was it to make that sacrifice?

Write or doodle your answer below.

Think about the sacrifice you drew or wrote about on the previous page.

Doodle the names of all
your friends & family who
connect to you & make you happy.

Draw or list your favorite things to do with your friends and family.

List 5 things they do that make you happy.

1.

2.

3.

4.

5.

Doodle your bucket list.

Doodle on this page when you are really angry.

What usually makes you angry?

Make a sign.
How do you feel when people ignore your signs?

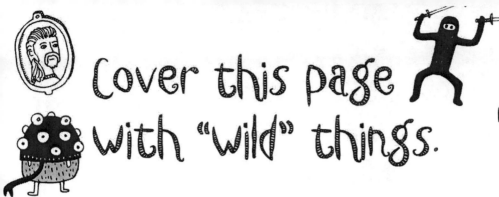

Cover this page with "wild" things.

Add five words that make you a free spirit

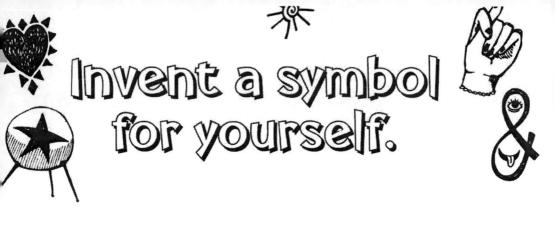

Invent a symbol for yourself.

What does it mean?

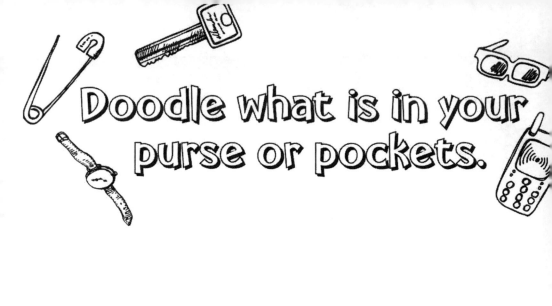

Doodle what is in your purse or pockets.

Write or doodle about the importance of the small stuff in your life.

Make your own code
and hide a secret message.

@$*#! @$*#!

Whenever you feel like using a
four-letter word, doodle your
frustrations here.

@$*#!

Trace your hand and make it into a turkey.

Write or doodle things you are thankful for.

Doodle the Calendar

Doodle your way through the Christian seasons of Advent, Christmas, Lent, and Easter, but be sure to save some creativity for the year's other big holidays and special occasions.

ADVENT AND CHRISTMAS

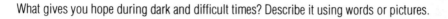

FIRST WEEK OF ADVENT: HOPE

What gives you hope during dark and difficult times? Describe it using words or pictures.

ADVENT AND CHRISTMAS

FIRST WEEK OF ADVENT: HOPE

Fill this page with words and/or pictures that represent sadness, despair, pain, stress, and fear. But don't put any of these words or pictures in the circle. After you've filled the rest of the page, draw or write something inside the circle that represents God's love through Jesus. How does Jesus offer hope to a hurting world?

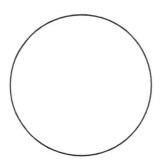

ADVENT AND CHRISTMAS

SECOND WEEK OF ADVENT: PEACE

This common symbol for peace originated as a combination of the semaphore signals for the letters "N" (for "nuclear") and "D" (for "disarmament").

Create your own symbol for peace, specifically the peace that God promises.

ADVENT AND CHRISTMAS

SECOND WEEK OF ADVENT: PEACE

Isaiah 11:1-9 provides a vision of God's peaceful kingdom, a world in which "The wolf will live with the lamb, and the leopard will lie down with the young goat" and "the calf and the young lion will feed together." Think of some other pairs of foes (human or animal) that will live together peacefully in God's kingdom.

ADVENT AND CHRISTMAS

THIRD WEEK OF ADVENT: JOY

When and where are you most joyful? Sketch this time and place using words or pictures.

ADVENT AND CHRISTMAS

THIRD WEEK OF ADVENT: JOY

In Jesus, God brought "joy to the world." How can you bring joy to the world, and especially to people who don't have a lot to be joyful about? Draw or write about ways that you can bring "joy to the world."

ADVENT AND CHRISTMAS

FOURTH WEEK OF ADVENT: LOVE

Medieval Christians adopted the heart symbol (see below) as a symbol of Jesus' love. The "sacred heart"—a heart that was both wounded and emitting beams of light—became common in Christian artwork. The heart symbol later came to represent love in general. Your challenge is to create a new symbol (or symbols) to represent love.

ADVENT AND CHRISTMAS

FOURTH WEEK OF ADVENT: LOVE

Fill this page with words, pictures, and symbols that represent God's love through Jesus Christ. Think about the love that God showed by sending Jesus to live among us; and think about how the love that came to earth on the first Christmas is still with us today.

ADVENT AND CHRISTMAS

CHRISTMAS

We often associate Christmas with giving and receiving gifts. Draw or write about some of the gifts you have given during this Advent and Christmas season. Do NOT include gifts that were wrapped and placed under a tree or given in a gift exchange.

ADVENT AND CHRISTMAS

CHRISTMAS

We often associate Christmas with giving and receiving gifts. Draw or write about some of the gifts you have received during this Advent and Christmas season. Do NOT include gifts that involved unwrapping packages or pulling things out of stockings.

ADVENT AND CHRISTMAS

NEW YEAR'S DAY

What were the five most important things that happened to you last year? Draw or write about them below.

ADVENT AND CHRISTMAS

NEW YEAR'S DAY

What is your prayer for the coming year? Doodle your prayer.

ADVENT AND CHRISTMAS

EPIPHANY

The magi, or wise men, brought young Jesus gifts of gold, frankincense, and myrrh (see Matthew 2:1-12). What are three gifts that you can offer to Jesus? Draw or doodle them below.

ADVENT AND CHRISTMAS

EPIPHANY

The magi's gift of gold has come to represent Jesus' royalty, since gold was a gift for kings. The smoke from frankincense rises toward God, so it has come to symbolize Jesus' divinity. Myrrh, which is used to anoint bodies for burial, has come to represent Jesus' humanity and sacrifice.

Think of some more contemporary symbols to represent Jesus' royalty (ruler of the world), divinity (one with God), and humanity (fully human) and draw them below.

royalty

divinity

humanity

LENT AND EASTER

ASH WEDNESDAY: REPENTANCE

Repentance begins with confession. Confess your sins using pictures. These pictures can be simple and don't have to make sense to anyone but you. You may confess recent sins or sins from weeks or months ago that are still on your mind.

LENT AND EASTER

ASH WEDNESDAY: REPENTANCE

Repentance involves not only confessing our sins but also turning away from them and moving in a new direction. Look at the pictures you drew on the previous page. For each sin picture, draw a picture below representing a positive behavior that could replace each sinful behavior. (For example, if you drew a picture representing stealing, you could draw a picture here to represent giving.)

LENT AND EASTER

FIRST SUNDAY OF LENT: TEMPTATION

In Matthew 4:1-11 Jesus is tempted three times. What tempts you? Draw pictures and symbols that represent these temptations.

LENT AND EASTER

FIRST SUNDAY OF LENT: TEMPTATION

Each time Jesus was tempted, he responded to the tempter by quoting Scripture. Who or what gives you strength when you're tempted? Draw or write about them. You might include some Scriptures that give you the strength to resist temptation.

LENT AND EASTER

SECOND SUNDAY OF LENT: FOLLOWING JESUS

Christians strive to follow Jesus, but where does Jesus lead us? To happiness? To justice and righteousness? To sacrifice? To eternal life? Draw a map across these two pages showing where we go when we follow Jesus.

LENT AND EASTER

SECOND SUNDAY OF LENT: FOLLOWING JESUS

Following Jesus requires us to follow the "directions" (Jesus' teaching). It also requires us to navigate obstacles that get in our way. Think about those things that make following Jesus difficult and mark them on your map.

LENT AND EASTER

THIRD SUNDAY OF LENT: FAITHFULNESS

A lot of things compete for our attention and keep us from being faithful to Jesus. Clear your mind of distractions by filling the page with a repetitive pattern.

LENT AND EASTER

THIRD SUNDAY OF LENT: FAITHFULNESS

Being faithful to Jesus means being committed to our relationship with Jesus. Draw a picture or symbol representing one way you've committed your life to Jesus.

LENT AND EASTER

FOURTH SUNDAY OF LENT: CALLING

What might God be calling you to do? Spend time in prayer considering God's call, then imagine a text-message conversation with God on the phone.

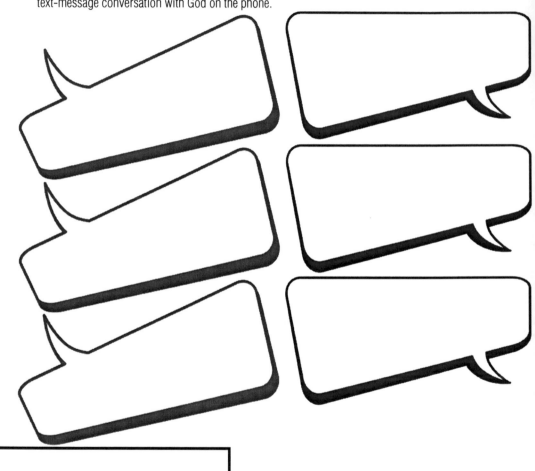

LENT AND EASTER

FOURTH SUNDAY OF LENT: CALLING

Before we discern what God is calling us to do, it is important that we identify the gifts God has given us. These gifts may include talents and abilities, privileges and opportunities, or resources (money and other stuff). Draw some of your gifts.

LENT AND EASTER

FIFTH SUNDAY OF LENT: DEVOTION

Devotion means being fully dedicated to a person, idea, or cause. As Christians we devote ourselves to God. But most likely you are—rightly or wrongly—devoted to some other people or things. Who or what (besides God) has earned your devotion?

LENT AND EASTER

FIFTH SUNDAY OF LENT: DEVOTION

Many Christians set aside personal devotional time: time spent praying, reading and reflecting on Scripture, and growing closer to God. Draw your ideal devotional space, a place where you can be alone with God and free from distractions.

LENT AND EASTER

PALM, OR PASSION, SUNDAY

The "Palm" in "Palm Sunday" refers to the branches that the crowds waved to celebrate Jesus' entry to Jerusalem. The "Passion" in "Passion Sunday" refers to Jesus' execution less than a week later. We don't know if the people celebrating Jesus' arrival were among the people demanding his crucifixion. But Jesus' situation changed quickly and dramatically. Draw a comic strip that shows a time when your fortunes changed suddenly.

LENT AND EASTER

PALM, OR PASSION, SUNDAY

On the first Palm Sunday people laid down their clothes for Jesus to ride over as he entered Jerusalem. Later in the week Jesus laid down his life to defeat sin and death. What can you "lay down," not just this week or during the season of Lent, but forever? Draw or write about these things below.

LENT AND EASTER

EASTER

Easter is all about hope. Because of the Resurrection, we need not fear death. Draw pictures or symbols of things that give you hope, or write the names of people who give you hope.

LENT AND EASTER

EASTER

In John 20:24-29 Jesus' disciple Thomas is reluctant to believe that Jesus has risen from the dead. He wants to see Jesus in person and touch his wounds. Jesus praises those who believe in him without firsthand physical evidence.

What signs have you seen that convince you that Jesus continues to live and work in our world? Draw or write about them below.

SPECIAL DAYS

MARTIN LUTHER KING, JR., DAY

In his "I Have a Dream" speech, Martin Luther King, Jr., quoted Amos 5:24, "Let justice roll down like waters, and righteousness like an ever-flowing stream." Amos and King had hope that the waters of justice would wash over injustice, oppression, and despair. Cover the page with examples of injustice, using pictures or words. Then "wash over" the page using marker, crayon, or paint to cover up the evil and brokenness.

SPECIAL DAYS

MARTIN LUTHER KING, JR., DAY

Martin Luther King, Jr., was a prophetic figure. Prophetic figures not only show people how a nation or community is broken but also give them a vision of how things could be better and more in line with God's will. Use the "broken" doodle below (the assorted lines and shapes) to create something better.

SPECIAL DAYS

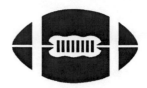

SUPER BOWL SUNDAY

Over the years Super Bowl commercials have become as much a spectacle as the game itself. Create a storyboard for a Super Bowl commercial advertising your church, the Bible, or Christianity in general.

SPECIAL DAYS

SUPER BOWL SUNDAY

For more than two decades churches have participated in the Souper Bowl of Caring to collect food and raise awareness about hunger on Super Bowl Sunday. Fill this page with pictures of foods that you could donate to help hungry persons or by making a shopping list. (You might even do research to find out what foods your local food bank needs.) When you're finished, put together a bag of food that you can donate.

SPECIAL DAYS

VALENTINE'S DAY

Who loves you? Draw hearts and mark them with the name, initials, or a symbol representing someone who loves you.

SPECIAL DAYS

VALENTINE'S DAY

The small, colored hearts featuring cute messages about love are one of the most popular Valentine's Day candies. Cover this page with small hearts and write on each one a message that describes God's love.

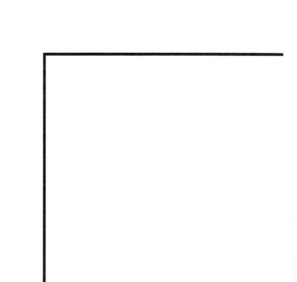

SPECIAL DAYS

NCAA TOURNAMENT

In the bracket below, list the eight things that are most important to you. If you had to eliminate one in each pair, which would you get rid of and which would you keep? Continue until only one item remains.

SPECIAL DAYS

NCAA TOURNAMENT

The hoopla surrounding NCAA Basketball Tournaments is called "March Madness" because of the passion of players, coaches, and fans and because so many crazy things—such as buzzer beaters and unknown teams upsetting national powers—tend to happen. Think of something that you're passionate about. Then doodle about that topic like a "mad" person.

SPECIAL DAYS

ST. PATRICK'S DAY

Tradition says that Patrick, the bishop in Ireland for whom St. Patrick's Day is named, used the three leaves of the shamrock to teach people about the Trinity. Draw a shamrock (or several shamrocks). Fill each leaf of the shamrock(s) with words, pictures, and symbols that describe God the Father, Jesus Christ, and the Holy Spirit.

SPECIAL DAYS

ST. PATRICK'S DAY

Patrick played a big role in the growth of Christianity in Ireland. He devoted his life to teaching the people of Ireland about Jesus and the Christian faith. In honor of Patrick, sketch a design for a poster, pamphlet, postcard, or website that tells people the good news of Jesus Christ.

Of course, posters and postcards alone won't do the work of teaching people about Jesus and the Christian faith. We also have to show people our faith through our love, our actions, our attitude, and our presence. Reflect on ways that you can use your entire being—words, actions, attitude, and love—to communicate Christ's message.

SPECIAL DAYS

MOTHER'S DAY AND FATHER'S DAY

Doodle your family tree. As much as you can, next to each family member's name, write or draw ways in which God has blessed that person.

SPECIAL DAYS

MOTHER'S DAY AND FATHER'S DAY

Exodus 20:12 says:

> Honor your father and mother so that your life will be long on the fertile land that the LORD your God is giving you.

Honor your parents, guardians, and/or other parental figures in your life by drawing or writing ways that you see God at work in them.

SPECIAL DAYS

PENTECOST

Peter told the crowd on Pentecost, "Change your hearts and lives." We can change our hearts and lives because of the Holy Spirit, who gives us peace, comfort, courage, strength, wisdom, and love. Below draw or write about a person whose heart has been transformed by the Holy Spirit. What sets this person apart or makes him or her different?

SPECIAL DAYS

PENTECOST

On the Day of Pentecost, all of the people gathered could understand the apostles when they spoke, even though they all spoke in different languages.

Write a message in code (for example, substitute numbers or symbols for letters or use words that stand for other words). Let other people try to decipher your code.

SPECIAL DAYS

PATRIOTIC HOLIDAYS

Write and draw ways that you observe God at work in your country (or state or province), including the ways that God works through individuals, groups, communities, and nature.

SPECIAL DAYS

PATRIOTIC HOLIDAYS

Draw a rough map of your country (or state or province). Mark on the map some ways that God has blessed the land in which you live. Also mark some needs that you see. Take these blessings and needs to God in prayer.

SPECIAL DAYS

HALLOWEEN

What masks do you wear? Lots of people wear masks and costumes for Halloween, but some of us wear masks and try to be someone we're not during other times of the year. How do you try to change the way people see you? Draw masks to show how you try to look for others.

SPECIAL DAYS

ALL SAINTS' DAY

All Saints' Day is the day on the Christian calendar when we remember those who have died during the previous year. Draw symbols representing—or write the names or initials of—people in your life who have died. They don't have to be people you knew personally, but can be anyone who had an impact on your life.

SPECIAL DAYS

THANKSGIVING

Doodle a cornucopia and fill it with blessings that make you thankful.

SPECIAL DAYS

THANKSGIVING

Earlier in the book you drew a hand turkey, a popular Thanksgiving activity. Trace your hand again below, but this time turn your hand into something other than a turkey that causes you to feel thankful.

Doodle Through Scripture

We encounter God in all sorts of ways in the pages of Scripture. Respond to the wisdom and truth of the Bible with pictures and scribbles.

OLD TESTAMENT HEROES

SHIPHRAH AND PUAH: EXODUS 1:15-21

Draw or write whatever comes to mind when you hear the word "brave." Think about what makes someone brave.

Read Exodus 1:15-21. Think about what made Shiphrah and Puah brave.

OLD TESTAMENT HEROES

MOSES: EXODUS 13:17-22

Moses led the people of Israel out of slavery in Egypt and toward the Promised Land. The people spent forty years winding through the wilderness before reaching their destination. Draw a winding path that twists and turns and covers this entire page. (You might create the path with a line, with sets of footprints, or with something else entirely.) When you are finished, trace the path with your finger and reflect on where God is leading you.

OLD TESTAMENT HEROES

GIDEON: JUDGES 6:17-23, 33-40

Gideon was surprised when God called him. He doubted God's intentions, he gave reasons why he was the wrong person for the job, and he tested God to make sure God was telling the truth.

If God were to call you to a task, what reasons would you give for why God shouldn't call you? Write or draw your answers.

1.

2.

3.

What are some reasons why God "should" choose you?

1.

2.

3.

OLD TESTAMENT HEROES

GIDEON: JUDGES 6:17-23, 33-40

Gideon twice asked God for a sign (Judges 6:17-23, 33-40), and God responded. What signs do you see of God's presence? Doodle the signs below, or doodle something that represents the signs you see.

OLD TESTAMENT HEROES

JOSIAH AND HULDAH: 2 KINGS 22:1–23:3

When the prophetess Huldah read from the Book of the Law found in the Temple, King Josiah realized that his kingdom had strayed from God. He responded by tearing his clothes and then making some big reforms. In honor of Josiah, tear this page. Then mend it with tape and make the page into something new and good by covering it in doodles.

OLD TESTAMENT HEROES

HERO!

JOSIAH AND HULDAH: 2 KINGS 22:1–23:3

The words that Huldah read from the Book of the Law found in the Temple completely changed the Kingdom of Judah. Find and read Bible verses that are meaningful to you, then write them on this page. Doodle around key words in the Scriptures.

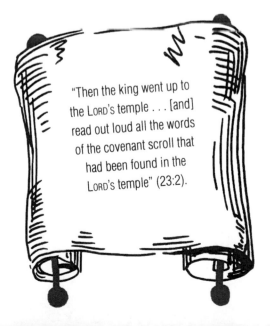

"Then the king went up to the LORD's temple . . . [and] read out loud all the words of the covenant scroll that had been found in the LORD's temple" (23:2).

OLD TESTAMENT HEROES HERO

JEREMIAH: JEREMIAH 1:4-10

When God called Jeremiah to be a "prophet to the nations" (Jeremiah 1:5), Jeremiah answered, "I don't know how to speak because I'm only a child" (1:6). God didn't accept Jeremiah's excuse and doesn't accept ours. If God were to call you to be a prophet, what excuses might you give?

I'm only a _____.

I'm only a _____.

I'm only a _____.

I'm only a _____.

OLD TESTAMENT HEROES

HERO!

JEREMIAH: JEREMIAH 18:1-11

Jeremiah learned that God is like a potter who can take clay that has fallen apart in his hands and create a new piece of pottery. We can make a similar comparison using paper.

Take scraps of paper—paper that has already been used for something else—and tear them into little pieces. Glue or tape the used, torn pieces of paper onto the page below to create a picture. Make something new and good out of something broken.

OLD TESTAMENT HEROES

DANIEL: DANIEL 1:1-21

When Daniel went to work for the king of Babylon, he refused the food offered to him. He believed eating it would violate the Old Testament law, so he requested vegetables instead. Daniel refused to compromise. Draw or write about something on which you refuse to compromise.

OLD TESTAMENT HEROES

HERO!

DANIEL: DANIEL 6:1-28

When Daniel violated a royal decree by praying to God instead of worshiping King Darius, the king reluctantly sentenced Daniel to death in a pit of lions. God "shut the lions' mouths" (Daniel 6:22), and they did not harm Daniel. What are some of the "lions" in your life? What would cause you trouble if you didn't have God's strength, guidance, and protection? Draw or write about these lions below.

PARABLES

MATTHEW 13:31-32

Jesus compared the kingdom of heaven to a mustard seed, a tiny seed that produces an enormous plant. God takes our small contributions and turns them into something greater. With that in mind, draw a seed in the middle of the page. Starting with the seed create a doodle, of a plant or something else, that covers the entire page.

PARABLES

MATTHEW 13:3-9, 18-23

In Matthew 13:3-9, 18-23 Jesus told a parable about seeds that landed on different soils. Seeds that landed on rocky ground, among thorny plants, or on a path didn't grow into healthy plants. But the seeds that landed on good soil thrived and produced fruit. Draw a plant that represents your faith. What helps your plant grow and stay healthy?

PARABLES

LUKE 15:1-7

Jesus told a parable about a shepherd who had one hundred sheep and lost one of them (see Luke 15:1-7). One out of one hundred doesn't seem like much, but the difference between all of the sheep and almost all of the sheep is significant. Draw one hundred of something, in ten rows of ten. Then "lose" one of the items by erasing it or marking it out. How does losing one of the one hundred affect the pattern?

PARABLES

LUKE 15:1-7

Create a doodle that fills this page. Hide a cross somewhere in the drawing. When you're finished, ask a friend to try to find the cross.

How much effort do you put into seeking out Jesus and God's will? What has God done to seek you out?

PARABLES

MATTHEW 25:14-30

Jesus told several parables involving money. Whenever we talk about money, we have to talk about value and how much things are worth. What would be worth $10 million to you? $1 million? Beside each amount below, write or draw something that is worth that amount of money to you.

$10 million

$1 million

$ 100 thousand

$ 10 thousand

$ 1,000

$ 100

PARABLES

MATTHEW 25:14-30

Jesus' parable of the talents (see Matthew 25:14-30) involves three servants, each of whom is entrusted with an amount of money. Regardless of how much money each servant receives, he is held accountable for how he uses the money. Draw or write about some of the things that God has entrusted to you. (This could include money, talents, opportunities, and so forth.)

PARABLES

LUKE 10:25-37

In the parable of the good Samaritan, the priest and Levite pass by on the road without helping the injured man. Make a map of some of the roads you travel each day. What needs do you encounter as you walk or drive on these roads? Draw on your map something that represents these needs.

PARABLES

LUKE 10:25-37

Jesus' parable of the good Samaritan was remarkable because his audience was Jewish, but the hero of the story was a Samaritan. Jews and Samaritans, who shared a common heritage but disagreed on certain religious matters, did not get along well together. Which groups today, like Jews and Samaritans in the first century, are at odds? Draw a fence or wall down the center of the page. Then, on opposite sides of the fence or wall, write the names of, or draw symbols representing, these groups.

PARABLES

LUKE 14:15-25

In Jesus' parable of the banquet, the host instructs his servants to "go to the highways and back alleys" and invite anyone and everyone they meet to attend his banquet. Invite anyone and everyone to draw a small picture or write a short message on one of these two pages. Allow them to draw or write anything. Try to get enough contributions to fill both pages.

PARABLES

LUKE 14:15-25

Continue your work from the previous page here. Think about how these pages are a representation of God's kingdom.

MIRACLES

JOHN 6:1-14

Jesus miraculously fed a multitude of five thousand people and then later fed another crowd of four thousand. If you had to feed thousands of people, what would you serve? Draw pictures of the items you'd prepare or create a menu.

MIRACLES

JOHN 6:1-14

In John's account of Jesus feeding the five thousand, a youth provides the five loaves and two fish that Jesus uses to feed the crowd. This young person's small offering made a big impact. Draw or list some small things that can make a big difference when offered up and blessed by God.

MIRACLES

MARK 2:1-12

The four friends described in Mark 2:1-12 had to overcome some obstacles to carry their friend to Jesus. In honor of their efforts, create a maze that is also difficult to navigate.

MIRACLES

MARK 2:1-12

Before Jesus empowered the paralyzed man in Mark 2:1-12 to walk again, he miraculously healed the man in a different way—by forgiving his sins. For what sins do you need to be healed and forgiven? Illustrate them below using pictures and symbols.

MIRACLES

LUKE 17:11-19

Jesus healed ten men who had a skin disease. Only one of the ten, a Samaritan, returned to thank Jesus. Create a thank-you card for someone you've forgotten to thank.

MIRACLES

MARK 1:29-34

Many of Jesus' miracles involved healing. Do you need to be healed of something? What? Healing isn't limited to physical ailments. Perhaps you need to be healed of greed or sadness or selfishness. Cover this page with adhesive bandages. On each one, write the name of something you want Jesus to heal.

MIRACLES

MARK 5:21-43

One of Jesus' greatest miracles was restoring the life of Jairus's daughter. In honor of this young girl, find some dead plant leaves. Give them "new life" by doing colorful leaf rubbings with a crayon.

MIRACLES

JOHN 11:1-4

When Jesus brought his friend Lazarus back to life, he showed that God is more powerful than even death, something that God demonstrated beyond all doubt through Jesus' resurrection. What are some other things over which God is more powerful? Complete and illustrate the statements below.

God is more powerful than . . .

God is more powerful than . . .

God is more powerful than . . .

MIRACLES

MARK 4:35-41

In Mark 4:35-41 Jesus and his disciples were on a boat during a terrible storm. Jesus was asleep, but his disciples woke him, afraid that they were in danger. Jesus stood up, calmed the storm, and asked his disciples why they were frightened.

Scribble on this page so that it looks like a storm hit it. Then "still the storm" by making a picture from the scribbles.

MIRACLES

MATTHEW 14:22-32

While Jesus' disciples were far from the shore, on a boat on Lake Gennesaret (the Sea of Galilee), Jesus walked out to them. Peter, who was frightened, said to Jesus, "Lord, if it's you, order me to come to you on the water" (Matthew 14:28). Peter was able to walk on the water until he became afraid and began to sink.

What amazing thing does fear keep you from doing? Draw it or write about it.

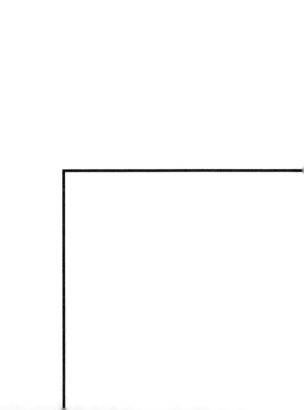

LESSER-KNOWN BIBLE STORIES

BALAAM'S DONKEY: NUMBERS 22:22-35

God used a talking donkey to get Balaam's attention. What would get your attention? Sketch this attention-getter below.

LESSER-KNOWN BIBLE STORIES

BALAAM'S DONKEY: NUMBERS 22:22-35

God used a donkey to communicate to Balaam, showing that God will talk to us in all sorts of ways. Listen in silence for God's voice. Draw what you hear God saying to you.

LESSER-KNOWN BIBLE STORIES

HEZEKIAH: 2 KINGS 18:1-7

Hezekiah may have been the greatest king in the history of the Kingdom of Judah. Among other things, he was known for removing from Judah all the altars and shrines to false gods.

Cover this page with pictures, words, and symbols of false gods we worship today (such as money, popularity, certain celebrities, and so forth). Then remove these gods by marking them out, erasing them, or turning them into things that can be used for God's glory.

LESSER-KNOWN BIBLE STORIES

HEZEKIAH: 2 KINGS 19:29–20:19

Some amazing and unbelievable things happened during Hezekiah's reign. God struck down the Assyrian army that was about to invade Judah. Then, when Hezekiah was on his death bed, God—through the prophet Isaiah—granted Hezekiah another fifteen years.

On the scale below, list eleven things that have happened to you, according to how incredible they were. For example, next to "0" write something that wasn't interesting at all, such as, "I brushed my teeth." Next to "10" write something so amazing that you can barely believe it happened.

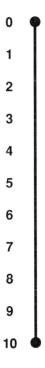

0

1

2

3

4

5

6

7

8

9

10

What makes the items you listed at 7, 8, 9, and 10 amazing? What, if anything, do these events tell you about God?

LESSER-KNOWN BIBLE STORIES

VALLEY OF THE DRY BONES: EZEKIEL 37:1-14

In Ezekiel 37:1-14 a bunch of dry bones come together to form skeletons. The skeletons are covered in flesh and skin and—after God breathes life into them—become people. God's ability to bring life from death was a sign of hope for the people of Judah, whose land and way of life had been taken from them.

Use dots to make an outline of a human figure. Invite a friend to connect the dots, then give your person clothes, a face, and other features.

LESSER-KNOWN BIBLE STORIES

VALLEY OF THE DRY BONES: EZEKIEL 37:1-14

A caterpillar, when it creates a cocoon, appears to die (even though it doesn't) but then later emerges as a butterfly. For this reason, the butterfly—like the bones that came to life in Ezekiel 37:1-14—is a common symbol of new life.

Create another symbol of new life that can give people hope when hope seems lost.

LESSER-KNOWN BIBLE STORIES

GOSPELS—SIMEON AND ANNA: LUKE 2:25-38

Even though we don't include them in nativity scenes, Simeon (an elderly and devout man in Jerusalem) and Anna (a prophetess) were among the first people to meet baby Jesus. Both waited many years to see the Messiah.

Is there something you've been waiting for a long time? Write or draw it below. Then use tally marks or some other method to show how many hours, days, or years you have waited.

Are you still waiting?

LESSER-KNOWN BIBLE STORIES

GOSPELS—JESUS' ARREST: MARK 14:43-51

When Jesus was arrested, things got chaotic. One of Jesus' followers pulled out a sword and cut off the ear of one of the high priest's servants. One disciple turned to run away. When someone grabbed the linen cloth he was wearing, he left the cloth behind and ran away naked. Only Jesus, through his resurrection days later, was able to restore order amid the chaos.

Using a pencil, create chaos by scribbling all over the page. Then use an eraser to create a symbol that represents Jesus in the midst of the chaos.

LESSER-KNOWN BIBLE STORIES

ACTS—SIMON THE MAGICIAN: ACTS 8:4-25

Simon the magician tried to buy the power of the Holy Spirit. The Spirit's power, of course, is not for sale. What are some powers that the Spirit has given you for free? Draw or doodle them below.

LESSER-KNOWN BIBLE STORIES

ACTS—EUTYCHUS: ACTS 20:7-12

The sermon that the apostle Paul preached in the town of Troas went on for so long that a young man named Eutychus drifted off to sleep and fell out the window to his death. Paul revived him, then kept on preaching.

What do you do when a sermon or talk is long (and boring)? Doodle below while your leader talks. Does the doodling help you focus? Does it become a distraction? Are your doodles inspired by the talk?

Doodle your faith

What do followers of Jesus believe? What do we do? Doodle your way through several core Christian beliefs, traditions, and practices.

WE BELIEVE

IN JESUS CHRIST

We profess Jesus as God but believe that, during his time on earth, he was also fully human. What does it mean to be fully human? Draw a stick figure or an outline of a person. Write or draw things on your person that show what you think it means for someone to be fully human.

WE BELIEVE

IN JESUS CHRIST

We believe that we know God most fully through the person of Jesus. So if we want to know about God's love, priorities, and expectations, we should look to Jesus' life, ministry, and example.

Draw below another stick figure or outline of a person. Write or draw things on your person to show how a person can follow Jesus' example.

WE BELIEVE

IN THE HOLY SPIRIT

Scripture calls the Holy Spirit the Advocate, Comforter, or Companion (depending on translation), and the Spirit of Truth. The Holy Spirit can be difficult to describe, but fire, wind, and a dove are common symbols for the Holy Spirit.

Draw a new symbol that represents what you know about the Holy Spirit and what the Holy Spirit does.

WE BELIEVE

IN THE HOLY SPIRIT

Often we become so wrapped up in our thoughts, our desires, and the distractions around us that we don't take time to listen for the Holy Spirit. Spend a few minutes in silence and pay attention to the Spirit. Write or draw anything that comes to mind. What might the Spirit be saying to you?

WE BELIEVE

THAT WE'RE CALLED TO BE THE CHURCH

The church is not a building; it is a collection of people, bound together by a love of and commitment to the God we know in Christ, with instructions to do God's work in the world. With that in mind, illustrate "the church" using pictures or words. (But don't draw or mention a building.)

WE BELIEVE

THAT WE'RE CALLED TO BE THE CHURCH

The apostle Paul calls the church the "body of Christ" and says that each of us is a part of the body (see 1 Corinthians 12:12-27). Which part are you? Are you an ear (good listener, hears the cries of people in need)? a hand (not afraid to do hard work or to reach out to people outside the church)? a foot (willing to go anywhere to do God's work)? What about others in your church? What parts of the body are they? Draw a human body below. Write your name, and the names of your friends and churchmates, on the appropriate body parts.

WE BELIEVE

IN GRACE THAT PRODUCES WORKS

Christians believe that we are saved by grace through Jesus Christ. Grace is something that is given freely, without price. Fill this page with blessings that God has given to you. Include things such as love, hope, and eternal life.

WE BELIEVE

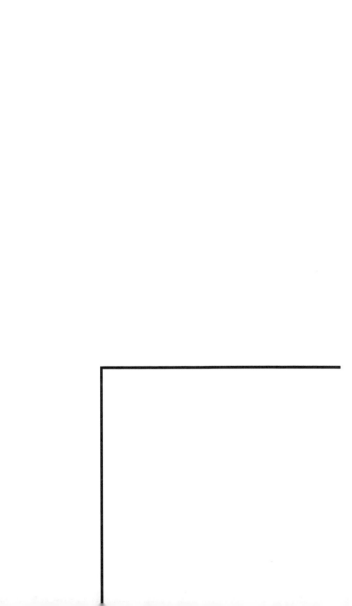

IN GRACE THAT PRODUCES WORKS

James writes that "faith without actions is dead" (James 2:26). When we accept God's grace, people should see our faith come to life in our actions. Draw or write what faith looks like when it's alive.

WE BELIEVE

IN THE RESURRECTION AND LIFE EVERLASTING

God promises to make all things new and offers us eternal life in God's new creation (see 2 Corinthians 5:17 and Revelation 21:1-5). What do you think God's new creation will look like? Sketch it below.

Look! I'm making all things new.
—Revelation 21:5

WE BELIEVE

IN THE RESURRECTION AND LIFE EVERLASTING

Jesus promises that we, like him, will experience resurrection and live eternally with God. What things in your life will last forever? What things in your life are only temporary? Draw or write below examples of each.

Temporary

Forever

WE DO

PRAY

What should we pray about? One way to structure our prayers is with the acronym ACTS, which stands for:

Adoration (praising God)

Confessing (bringing our sins before God)

Thanksgiving (thanking God for the ways in which we are blessed)

Supplication (praying for our needs and the needs of others)

Compose your "ACTS" prayer below by jotting down your praises, confessions, reasons to be thankful, and concerns about needs that you know about or have seen.

WE DO

PRAV

Doodle your prayer to God below.

WE DO

ACTS OF MERCY AND JUSTICE

Name below, using words, pictures, or symbols, five needs that you see in your community.

WE DO

ACTS OF MERCY AND JUSTICE

Look at the list of needs you wrote about or sketched on the previous page. Then sketch (or describe in words) one way you can respond to one of these needs. Afterward make a plan to put your sketch into action.

WE DO

WORSHIP

Sketch your church's worship space. Talk to leaders in your congregation about why your worship space is arranged in a certain way.

WE DO

WORSHIP

What would your ideal worship service be like? Describe the service using pictures or words. (Christian worship usually follows a pattern of: 1—entrance and gathering; 2—reading, proclaiming, and responding to God's Word; 3—giving thanks and taking Holy Communion; 4—sending forth.)

WE DO

GIVING GENEROUSLY

When we talk about giving, we often think about money. What, besides money, do you have that you can generously give to the church? Draw these gifts below.

WE DO

GIVING GENEROUSLY

Think of eleven of your possessions that would be hard for you to give away. List these items below on a scale of 0 to 10, with "0" being something you would give away without even thinking about it and "10" being something you would never give away.

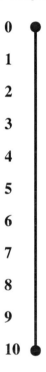

0

1

2

3

4

5

6

7

8

9

10

Giving generously means not only giving 0's, 1's, and 2's but also being willing to part with 8's, 9's, and 10's.

WE DO

BAPTISM AND COMMUNION

Splash water droplets, or doodle them, on this page as a way to remind you of your baptism or to look forward to your baptism.

If you have been baptized, when and where did your baptism take place? Who was there?

WE DO

BAPTISM AND COMMUNION

During his final meal with his disciples before his death, Jesus instructed us to break bread and drink from the cup as a way of remembering him (see 1 Corinthians 11:23-26). What are some things that you remember about Jesus? Draw and/or write some of your memories below.

On the night on which he was betrayed, the Lord Jesus took bread. After giving thanks, he broke it and said, "This is my body, which is for you; do this to remember me." He did the same thing with the cup, after they had eaten, saying, "This cup is the new covenant in my blood. Every time you drink it, do this to remember me."

—1 Corinthians 11:23b-25

Doodle the Bible

How do you picture the events and people of the Bible? Sketch some scenes from the Old and New Testaments.

DOODLE THE BIBLE

Draw the Scripture below as you picture it. (You may want to look up and read the Scripture to put it in context.)

"The Lᴏʀᴅ's messenger appeared to [Moses] in a flame of fire in the middle of a bush. Moses saw that the bush was in flames, but it didn't burn up."—Exodus 3:2

DOODLE THE BIBLE

Draw the Scripture below as you picture it. (You may want to look up and read the Scripture to put it in context.)

"The style of chariot driving is like Jehu, Nimshi's son. Jehu drives like a madman."—2 Kings 9:20b

DOODLE THE BIBLE

Draw the Scripture below as you picture it. (You may want to look up and read the Scripture to put it in context.)

"Each [winged creature] had six wings: with two they veiled their faces, with two their feet, and with two they flew about. . . . Then one of the winged creatures flew to me, holding a glowing coal that he had taken from the altar with tongs. He touched my mouth and said, 'See, this has touched your lips. Your guilt has departed, and your sin is removed.'"—Isaiah 6:2b, 6-7

DOODLE THE BIBLE

Draw the Scripture below as you picture it. (You may want to look up and read the Scripture to put it in context.)

"Jesus took Peter, James, and John his brother, and brought them to the top of a very high mountain. He was transformed in front of them. His face shone like the sun, and his clothes became as white as light."—Matthew 17:1-2

DOODLE THE BIBLE

Draw the Scripture below as you picture it. (You may want to look up and read the Scripture to put it in context.)

"When Pentecost Day arrived, they were all together in one place. Suddenly a sound from heaven like the howling of a fierce wind filled the entire house where they were sitting. They saw what seemed to be individual flames of fire alighting on each one of them. They were all filled with the Holy Spirit."
—Acts 2:1-4a

DOODLE THE BIBLE

Draw the Scripture below as you picture it. (You may want to look up and read the Scripture to put it in context.)

"Then the angel showed me the river of life-giving water, shining like crystal, flowing from the throne of God and the Lamb through the middle of the city's main street. On each side of the river is the tree of life, which produces twelve crops of fruit, bearing its fruit each month. The tree's leaves are for the healing of the nations."—Revelation 22:1-2

Top five Lists

What are your favorite things and what do they say about you? Make some lists and reflect on how God works through your interests and gifts.

TOP 5 LISTS

What are your five favorite movies?

1.

2.

3.

4.

5.

What does your choice of movies say about your faith and your relationship with God?

TOP 5 LISTS

Sketch a scene or character from
one of your five favorite movies.

TOP 5 LISTS

What are your five favorite songs?

1.

2.

3.

4.

5.

What does your choice of music say about your faith and your relationship with God?

TOP 5 LISTS

Listen to one of your five favorite songs and doodle what you hear in the lyrics.

Sing to the LORD, all the earth!

—*1 Chronicles 16:23*

TOP 5 LISTS

Which five books have had the biggest impact on your life?

1.

2.

3.

4.

5.

What made each book so important to you?

TOP 5 LISTS

Sketch a scene or character from one of the books that has had the biggest impact on your life.

If all of your favorite books are nonfiction, illustrate one thing that you have learned from one of your favorite books.

TOP 5 LISTS

What are your five favorite games (sports, videogames, board games, and so on)?

1.

2.

3.

4.

5.

TOP 5 LISTS

Create a game or puzzle below.

TOP 5 LISTS

What are your five favorite foods?

1.

2.

3.

4.

5.

TOP 5 LISTS

Sketch your favorite meal.

TOP 5 LISTS

What are your five favorite animals?

1.

2.

3.

4.

5.

TOP 5 LISTS

As God filled the world with animals,
fill this page with animals—real animals and/or imaginary
animals that you create.

TOP 5 LISTS

What are your five favorite inventions or gadgets?

1.

2.

3.

4.

5.

TOP 5 LISTS

Design your own gadget or invention.
Think about what it does, how it makes
life easier, and how it could be used to serve God
and others.

TOP 5 LISTS

Name five gifts that God has given you.

1.

2.

3.

4.

5.

TOP 5 LISTS

Sketch at least one way that you can use one or more of the five gifts you listed on the previous page.

TOP 5 LISTS

Think of five people who have extraordinary gifts that you admire. List them and their gifts.

1.

2.

3.

4.

5.

TOP 5 LISTS

Sketch one of the people you listed on the previous page as a superhero.

Think about what heroic things he or she has done or could do with his or her gifts. Think of ways he or she could use these gifts in service to God and others.

> *I assure you that whoever believes in me will do the works that I do. They will do even greater works than these.*
>
> *—John 14:12*

TOP 5 LISTS

List five places where you feel closest to God. Why do you feel close to God in these places?

1.

2.

3.

4.

5.

TOP 5 LISTS

Sketch one of the places where you feel closest to God.

TOP 5 LISTS

List five needs that you see in your community.

1.

2.

3.

4.

5.

TOP 5 LISTS

Sketch one way you can respond to one or more of these needs.

CPSIA information can be obtained at www.ICGtesting.com
Printed in the USA
LVOW11s1927170315

430945LV00007B/290/P